Arthur

Hope this book brings you as much pleasure as you have given me during my stay in Bradford, April 1987. It was lovely to have the opportunitie to relive some of my youth and see dear friends again.

With grateful thanks much love

Liz

Bradford in old picture postcards

by
Gary Firth

European Library - Zaltbommel/Netherlands MCMLXXXIV

To my dear wife Jackie

GB ISBN 90 288 2642 4

European Library in Zaltbommel/Netherlands publishes among other things the following series:

IN OLD PICTURE POSTCARDS *is a series of books which sets out to show what a particular place looked like and what life was like in Victorian and Edwardian times. A book about virtually every town in the United Kingdom is to be published in this series. By the end of this year about 175 different volumes will have appeared. 1,250 books have already been published devoted to the Netherlands with the title* **In oude ansichten.** *In Germany, Austria and Switzerland 500, 60 and 15 books have been published as* **In alten Ansichten;** *in France by the name* **En cartes postales anciennes** *and in Belgium as* **En cartes postales anciennes** *and/or* **In oude prentkaarten** *150 respectively 400 volumes have been published.*

For further particulars about published or forthcoming books, apply to your bookseller or direct to the publisher.

This edition has been printed and bound by Grafisch Bedrijf De Steigerpoort in Zaltbommel/Netherlands.

INTRODUCTION

The greater part of the photographs and picture post-cards in this pictorial record of Bradford originate in the decades on either side of the First World War, when Bradford was still the classic Victorian city, having expanded from a small semi-rural township (population 13,264 in 1801) at the beginning of the nineteenth century to one of Britain's largest urban communities as early as 1851. Population expansion eased after 1871 by which time the city housed almost 150,000 inhabitants. Many of those people had found work in the worsted textile trade which, after 1874, experienced a series of setbacks to the seemingly inexorable forward march of the earlier decades. The town's iron-making tradition was also rocked in these years when, in 1898, the Bowling Ironworks went into liquidation.

The Bradford of these pictures was, therefore, having to make minor adjustments to its traditional industrial and economic framework. New kinds of employment appeared, as there was an increasing call for the services of professionals and specialists as well as a proliferation of public sector employees, such as clerks, secretaries, and a whole range of municipal workers in public transport and public health. Also, the retailing revolution in the high street threw up an unprecedented number of small shopkeepers, who began to take their place in the running of the town's affairs in place of the traditional textile magnates, many of whom were beginning to transfer their capital and their interests out of the town. Others too, were deserting the inner city as thousands of middle-class folk moved out to live in the suburbs of Bingley and Ilkley, thanks to the growth of an urban transportation system of horse buses and steam trams after 1882.

The city's long established links with Nonconformity, particularly the Congregationalists and Baptists, was under threat from spectator sports and mass leisure pursuits like football, cycling and, later, cinema, in addition to the long-standing public house and music hall. Another attack upon Bradford's religious standing came through the establishment of a state education system in 1870 and its sequel the 1902 Education Act which ended the Bradford School Board and placed the city's educational organisation under the Education Committee of a County Borough. The town, in the years before the First World War, was active in the municipal provision of educational welfare, school meals, school clinics, as well as schools for the mentally and physically handicapped. Nor was the city culturally backward in those years. One Bradfordian of that era who spent his youth in the city was later to write:

Bradford of these years was no ordinary city... In those pre 1914 days Bradford was considered the most progressive place in the United Kingdom. The Independent Labour Party was born in Bradford. Our Friday Subscription Concerts were famous; in addition we had our permanent symphony orchestra and two magnificent choral societies... we had two theatres, two music halls, two or three professional concert parties, a flourishing arts club, three daily papers and a weekly. (John Boynton Priestley, 1946.)

J.B. Priestley's Bradford has almost disappeared into the past but perhaps this small collection of street scenes and characters might prompt a fascinating reminiscence, a chance glimpse from some bank of the memory which will make the Bradford of Victorian times live again.
The author, Dr. Gary Firth, was born in Shipley, near Bradford and educated at Bingley Grammar School and Leeds University. He obtained his doctorate from the University of Bradford in 1974 while teaching history in Bradford secondary schools. He is, at present, a Principal Lecturer at Bradford & Ilkley Community College. He writes, lectures and broadcasts on Bradford's industrial past.

The author would like to thank, by way of acknowledgement, the following for their permission to reproduce photographs in this book:
Mrs. Burrows, Mrs. Bruce, David Burnet, Keith Davies, Bradford Central Library, Bradford Telegraph & Argus and in particular Christopher and David Pratt for allowing me to make use of their father's fine collection of negatives. My thanks also go to Hilda Watkinson for typing assistance and to Gordon Yates for his photographic expertise.
A special thank you to Michael Atkinson for his enthusiasm for and detailed knowledge of, the photographs in this book.

G. Firth
Bradford & Ilkley Community College

1. *Bradford in 1820.* A painting of Bradford from the north-west showing the old settlement sitting in a natural amphitheatre of rolling hills and green pastures. The chimneys of the early textile mills are beginning to sprout along the line of the Bradford Beck and Canal (foreground). The left of the picture is dominated by the ancient Parish Church while to the right is the more modern edifice of Christ Church (1813) which was located at the top of Darley Street and was eventually pulled down in 1879 for street improvements.

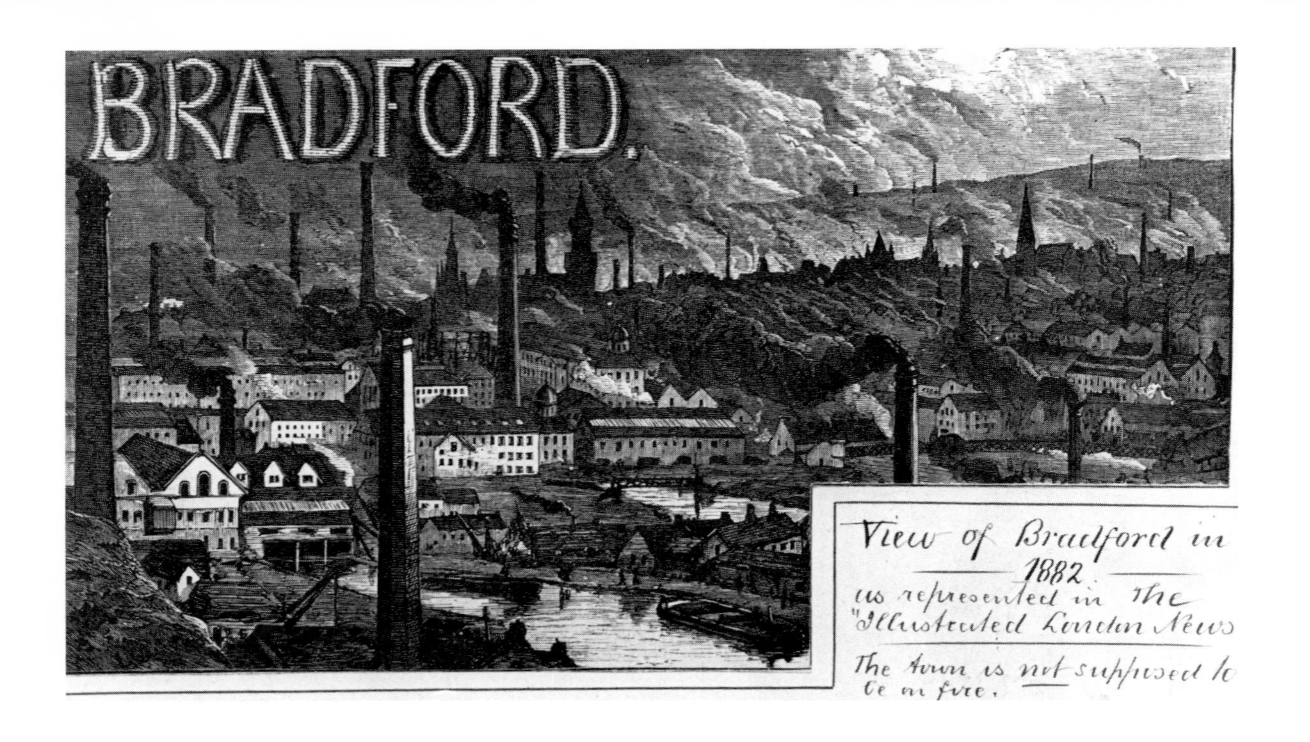

2. *Bradford 1882.* This is a very different view of the town taken from the Illustrated London News of 1882, showing the Victorian city after eight decades of industrialism. A sulphurous pall of smoke hovered over the centre of the city, blotting out the natural light and bringing with it numerous health hazards for inhabitants. In the foreground, the Bradford Canal (1774) and the 'Mucky Beck' run side by side, both of them notorious open sewers and receptacles for every form of filth.

3. *Market Street 1910.* Formerly known as New Street, it was completely transformed by the civic rebuilding programme after 1860. The regular Italianate style of the buildings from Bank Street to the Town Hall was dominated by the elegant Venetian Gothic style of the Wool Exchange left of centre of the photograph. Beneath that building was the stained-glass palace of Blake's drinking house and restaurant. On the immediate left can be seen a corner of Brown & Muff's store.

4. *Market Street circa 1900.* Obviously cleared of traffic for the benefit of the photograph by the beefy figure at bottom left. In the centre of the photograph can be seen the relatively new and lavish emporium of Brown & Muffs, opened in 1871 and for many years the finest and largest department store of its kind in West Yorkshire.

5. *Market Street 1920.* Another view of this fine Victorian thoroughfare from Forster Square.

6. *Kirkgate circa 1890.* A fine view of Bradford's busy shopping and marketing thoroughfare. To the right is the Kirkgate entrance to the Market (built 1866-1871). This impressive entrance, well remembered by many Bradfordians, was dominated by the carved figures of Flora and Pomona, the goddesses of flowers and fruit. It can still be seen at the Bradford Industrial Museum, Eccleshill. In the centre of the photograph is the tea warehouse of Brooke, Bond & Co.

7. *Darley Street.* This district was originally part of the manorial estate, that is the gardens, orchards and rockery. It is thought to have been named after Darley Hall, seat of the manor lord. It had a reputation in 1900 for being the city's most fashionable thoroughfare.

8. *Westgate 1920.* Another of Bradford's original highways, Westgate's status as a residential area diminished as the town expanded after 1820. This view from the top of Ivegate is dominated by the Central Coffee Tavern and Hotel. Numerous public houses, including the Pack Horse, Adelphi, Boy & Barrel and Star Inn, were a feature of higher Westgate. On the left is Mr. A. Altham's tea shop renowned for free gifts of teapots, flowerstands and workboxes.

9. *Tyrrel Street 1891.* From the junction with Sunbridge Road looking towards Bank Street and Hustlergate. To the left are the impressive premises of George Thorp (1876), Bradford's most successful draper of the Victorian times. In the centre (tower) are the premises of the Bradford Commercial Bank, Hustlergate (1868) now occupied by the National Westminster Bank. On the extreme right of the photograph at 29, Tyrrel Street, is Butterfields whose premises continue as opticians.

10. *Tyrrel Street 1907.* A later and much busier photograph of Tyrrel Street taken from a spot nearer the Town Hall than in the previous picture. On the left the Orient Café adjoins the Empress Hotel owned by Francis Laidler, who later opened the Alhambra as a variety theatre in 1914.

11. *Manningham Lane and North Parade, circa 1904.* With the demolition of Christ Church in 1879, Darley Street was carried through to North Parade which had been given its name fifty years before. At Fountain Street, North Parade merged with Manningham Lane which was the chief promenade of the town, particularly since the opening of Lister Park. The Yorkshire Penny Bank, built in 1895, dominates the centre of the second photograph.

12. *Manningham Lane, circa 1900.* Another view along Manningham Lane at the junction with Manor Lane. On the far left is the post office and stationery business of Tom Clegg. Next door, the fancy drapery emporium of Sykes & Son. Beyond, on the same side of the street, is the Royal Arcade. To the right, a familiar sight to all Bradfordians at this time, a cart ladened with wool bales.

13. *Forster Square circa 1910.* These two photographs are dominated by the statue of Richard Oastler, the 'Factory King'. It was unveiled in May 1869 by the 7th Earl of Shaftesbury. The bronze figures of Oastler and the two factory children moved Margaret McMillan to tears as she stepped out of the railway station on her first visit to Bradford.

14. *Advertising in Forster Square, 1912.* Before the age of the 'commercial break', stores advertised themselves and their goods in a variety of ways. John S. Driver, general grocer and greengrocer, certainly goes to great lengths in this pre-1914 sales campaign. From their headquarters in Ingleby Road, and their numerous branches around Bradford, John S. Driver supplied cheap but quality goods. During the hard times of the inter-war years thousands were thankful for the 'Driver Parcel' of a rabbit, one onion, a carrot, a small turnip and a few potatoes, all for a shilling!

15. *Town Hall.* This is Bradford's contribution of the wave of civic pride which swept mid-Victorian England. The building was designed by a firm of Bradford architects, Lockwood & Mawson, whose mediaeval Gothic style set the architectural 'tone' for much of the city. The elegant Italianate campanile of over 200 feet makes an impressive landmark to the city skyline.

16. *Laying of the foundation stone, Bradford Town Hall 1870.* The Bradford Council, in 1870, finally accepted the tender of John Ives & Son of Shipley for the new town hall building. A month later, the foundation stone was laid amid great ceremony. Local dignitaries, headed by the Mayor, Alderman Mark Dawson, marched in procession to the site which was surrounded by platforms, barriers and an enormous gallery on the Chapel Lane side, all full of people. The Mayor laid the foundation stone (north-east corner of the tower) with a silver gilt trowel presented to him by Matthew Thompson.

17. *Town Hall Square 1895.* The building with the bow front to the left of the picture is the George Hotel at the end of Market Street, where mine host was Tommy Wood. The Square is dominated by the distinct Gothic style of the Town Hall clock tower.

18. *Town Hall Square circa 1910.* A fine photograph of city life just before the First World War. The hustle and bustle of Market Street provides a busy backcloth to Town Hall Square, the terminus for several electrically-driven tram services including this one to Queensbury. The crowd of people to the right are awaiting a tram in specially provided stations. The building in the centre of the photograph is the Refreshment House of the Bradford Coffee Tavern Company.

19. *Town Hall Square, circa 1904.* This is also part of the Mechanics' Institute building at the junction of Tyrrel Street (extreme left) and Manchester Road (front). This fine block also housed the Provincial Building Society. Queues for trams (centre) only became a feature of Bradford streets after the introduction of electric traction in 1898. Hithertoo there were no official 'stops'.

20. *Manchester Road and the royal visit 1904.* Two views of the celebrations at the city end of Manchester Road as it joins with Tyrrel Street and Little Horton Lane, on the occasion of the visit of the Prince and Princess of Wales to unveil the statue of Queen Victoria in 1904.

21. *Tyrrel Street, circa 1908.* If the wind was in the right direction one could catch the aroma of freshly ground coffee from Collinson's on every day of the week except Sunday. The fascinating shop window, with its numerous blends of coffee and oriental teas, attracted many a passer-by and even tempted them inside, to the delights of coffee and cakes, and even a three piece orchestra. The 129 tram on the busy Thornton Road service is one of the municipal steam trams first introduced in 1882 but superseded by electric traction after 1898.

22. *General Post Office, Forster Square.* Opened in September 1887 after a lengthy period of construction due to bad weather and building strikes. It immediately held centre stage in Bradford's new urban focus of Forster Square.

23. *General Post Office by moonlight.* A photographic trick much practised by the commercial photographers, Fenwicks of York. The photograph was probably taken at 11.45 a.m. and a moon added quite arbitrarily.

24. Two contrasting minor Bradford highways, Charles Street (above) dominated by the gloomy and oppressive warehouse blocks. Below, the more traditional Bradford street of Barkerend Road with its diminutive cottages and the ancient Paper Hall.

25. *Peel Square circa 1890.* Peel's statue was an expression of gratitude from Bradford's men of commerce for the free-trade policy implemented by that statesman. Surrounded by the profusely carved warehouses of Charles Street, Hall Ings and Leeds Road (left), the statue was unveiled in November 1855 in the presence of the sculptor William Behnes. Since 1957 the statue has been located in Peel Park.

26. *John Wood.* Born in 1793 John Wood entered the Bradford worsted trade at the age of nineteen setting up his own combing and spinning business. Within twenty years he was the town's largest employer. He ran a factory school for 500 children and financed many local charities. As an Anglican Tory he was a founding father of the Ten Hour Movement. His fortune made, Wood gradually handed on his business to his half cousin William Walker. By 1855 John Wood had bought himself into the ranks of the Hampshire squirearchy. This photograph was taken shortly before his death in 1871.

27. *The Salt Statue, 1888.* The statue had pride of place in front of the new town hall until it caused traffic congestion in the 1890's. It was erected in Salt's lifetime, as a tribute from the people of Bradford and Saltaire. A public holiday was declared when it was unveiled by the Duke of Devonshire in 1874. It was moved to Lister Park in the summer of 1896.

28. *Parish Church, North Side, circa 1900.* In these photographs the mills, warehouses and operatives' cottages of industrial Bradford surround the town's ancient parish church and its graveyard. This is the third church built on this site. The first is said to have dated from the seventh century. A Norman church built 1200 A.D. was destroyed by the Scots almost a century later. The tower, which served Bradfordians well during the civil war, was added at the beginning of the sixteenth century. Under Dr. Scoresby and Dr. Burnet the interior of the church was completely transformed to provide its present imposing grandeur. It became a cathedral in 1918.

29. *Lapage Street, 1908.*

30. *Jubilee Fire, Horton, 1897.* This enormous pile at Revey Beacon was the City of Bradford's Municipal Jubilee bonfire. Queen Victoria's Diamond Jubilee coincided with the golden jubilee of Bradford's status as a municipality. The Council, mindful of the town's phenomenal growth in the intervening years, petitioned the Queen to raise Bradford to the rank of a city. Thus Bradfordians had cause to enjoy a double celebration in the summer of 1897.

31. *Coronation celebrations, Norwood Green, 1902.* The Victorian age ended 22nd January 1901 with the death of the old queen. King Edward's coronation was postponed until the summer of 1902, owing to his illness. Norwood Green's coronation celebrations took place on Saturday 9th August of that year, when a procession of school children and the Parish Council were accompanied to Field Head Farm by the Brighouse and Raistrick Temperance Brass Band. The children of the village enjoyed side-shows and rides on two decorated motor cars. They were given coronation mugs followed by an enormous bunfight at the School. In the evening their parents roasted a sheep and toasted the health of the new king. The Edwardian era had begun.

32. *The Park Gates, Manningham Park.* We see here the junction of Manningham Lane and Oak Lane at the beginning of the twentieth century. Street Cars were first run from Darley Street to Manningham Park Gates in 1882. These were horse-drawn cabs which worked on a half-hourly service provided by a private company which leased the track from the Corporation. The Park, Lister Park, was purchased by the city fathers for £40,000 from Lord Masham in 1870. Just inside the park gates can be seen the statue of Samuel Cunliffe Lister.

33. *Manningham Old Hall* was erected by Samuel Lister in 1769 and passed to E.C. Lister by marriage in 1821. His son Samuel Cunliffe Lister, the textile magnate, made several structural changes whilst in residence. The building was demolished in 1898 in order to erect the Cartwright Memorial Hall. The house and several servants were badly damaged when lightning struck the house during a storm in 1821.

34. *Band stand, Lister Park, circa 1914.* The Sunday stroll around the park was sweetened by the strains of a slow melody played by any one of dozens of local brass bands. Here was a 'cultural and class mix' where no self-respecting artisan would be seen in his clogs; the cloth cap gave way once a week to the best suit and 'billy cock' hat.

35. *Bowling Park, 1889.* Fifty-three acres of land, adjoining the property of Abraham Mitchell, were bought by the Corporation and laid out as a public park in September 1880, at a cost of £47,000. As can be seen from this photograph, the park is bounded on one side by the historic mansion of Bolling Hall. The designers of the park were Kershaw & Hepworth of Brighouse.

36. *Junction of Kirkgate and Ivegate.* The meeting here of two of Bradford's ancient thoroughfares, Kirkgate, to the left of the photograph and Ivegate, sloping away to the right. The building in the centre originally served the citizens of Bradford as a court of justice, the Hall of Pleas and later as a Toll Bar. Here also was housed the town's dungeon, where the early Methodist preacher, John Nelson was briefly incarcerated in 1744, the same year that John Wesley made his first visit to Bradford.

37. *Killing Hall Road, circa 1902.*

38. *Old Infirmary*. This is the dispensary entrance to the Old Infirmary in Westgate. The dispensary itself was opened in 1873 but the main building of the Infirmary was opened for in-patients in 1843 and was considerably extended twenty years later. The mock Tudor style of the original building was followed in all subsequent extensions including a new wing in 1885. Twelve years later Queen Victoria gave permission for the hospital to be named the Bradford Royal Infirmary.

39. *Bolton Woods Quarry circa 1910.* In 1853 two working men, John Holmes and Thomas Dawson, came to an agreement with Mr. Barton of Bolton Hall, concerning the quarrying of stone at Bolton Woods. It was the beginning of a lucrative business, for the millowners of the West Riding were demanding fine quality ashlar for their multistorey mills and warehouses. The fine sandstone from Gaisby was used in many of Bradford's public and commercial buildings as well as those of other cities throughout Britain. In this photograph, best stone (up to ten feet thick) is being cut by Waterhouse, Denbigh & Company, subsequent owners of the quarries.

40. *Bradford Moor Barracks 1870.* It was here that a company of the 5th Dragoon Guards was stationed throughout the 1840's when physical-force Chartism was at its height in the area. In the half century after 1884 the barracks were occupied successively by the Green Howards, 70th West Riding Brigade Royal Artillery and the Royal Army Service Corps. The site of the barracks is now occupied by the premises of a large engineering company.

41. *Privy middens.* At the end of the nineteenth century a large number of working people in Bradford lived in accommodation like this, offering one room upstairs, one down and a windowless cellar. At the rear of the house (usually back to back) was the privy midden, for every kind of refuse, and often serving up to four households. Opening the ashpit doors the night soil men shovelled the refuse onto the cobbled yards and into the carts. The mess and stench they left behind, encouraged summer houseflies and bluebottles swarmed in every kitchen. Only the swilling and scrubbing of overworked housewives, broken like horses, kept disease and unpleasantness at bay.

42. *Poole Alley.* One of hundreds of alleys or 'ginnels' leading to the courts or yards of the early Victorian city. This one was located off Silsbridge Lane, an area noted for its high proportion of Irish immigrants. It was in narrow and unhealthy quarters like this that early town dwellers tried to continue their rural way of life and raise pigs, hens, etc.

43. *Smiddles Lane.* Taken about 1910 looking from Smiddles Lane towards Southfield Lane in the distance.

44. *Esholt Village.* This village remains a quiet rural backwater close to the inner city of Bradford. These seventeenth century cottages form part of the Esholt Hall estate formerly the site of a small Cistercian nunnery.

45. *Kirkgate 1891.* This fine building is fronted by the junction of Bradford's three most ancient highways, Ivegate, Westgate (bottom left) and Kirkgate (bottom right). The ground floor architecture masked by the shop front of the premises of Manoah Rhodes, jewellers. The remaining storeys are clearly expressed by a firm string course or, in the case of the first floor, by a shallow balcony. The building is very much in the Italianate style of several of Bradford's public buildings. The windows are styled differently on each floor and the top of the façade is crowned with a bold cornice and balustrade.

46. *Lower Kirkgate 1877.* Front right are the premises of Becket & Company who established their banking concern in Bradford in 1833 having commenced business in Leeds as early as 1758. These premises were rebuilt by Beckets in 1888. In the distance on the left hand side of the street can be seen the distinctive 'hound' fronting the premises of the original Talbot Hotel. Directly opposite was the old Post Office and the premises of the Bradford Banking Company.

47. *Old Talbot Hotel, Kirkgate, circa 1880.* In the early decades of the nineteenth century this ancient hostelry was the headquarters of the Bradford Tories and was patronised by such famous 'blues' as E.C. Lister and Frank Duffield. It was one of the town's great coaching houses, the 'Union' calling here daily on its runs from Leeds to Kendal. The hotel was considerably rebuilt in 1879/80.

48. *Westgate 1891.* Looking down Westgate towards the junction with Kirkgate and Ivegate. On the right the premises of another famous Bradford jeweller, Fattorinis. In the distance the premises of Waller & Sons, situated at the top of Ivegate and adjoining Millergate.

49. *Mechanics Institute circa 1885.* This fine classical building was located between Tyrrel Street, Bridge Street and Market Street. The building is of four storeys the uppermost storey being part of the roof. On the ground floor were shop premises and the upper floors housed the Bradford Mechanics Institute (founded 1832) whose guests included Thackeray, Ruskin and many other Victorian 'literati'. The façade of the building is dominated by the range and symmetry of its many windows. It was crowned by a heavy but symmetrical cornice which was in turn topped by a number of chimney stacks which gave an untidy appearance to the roof-top. The building was opened in 1871 and demolished one hundred years later.

50. *Frizinghall 1860.* Perhaps the oldest photograph in this book. This is a rare view of Frizinghall at the junction of Buxton Lane with Frizinghall Lane taken in 1860. The break in the wall in Buxton Lane is the site of the spring-water well. The photographer was positioned at an old farmhouse called the Old Castle, although there was nothing castellated about it.

51. *Toller Lane.* Travelling on the open topped tram on a summer's day through the sylvan beauty of Toller Lane (before it joins with Smith Lane and Duckworth Lane), was a pleasant experience for the price of a copper or two.

52. *The Old Crown, Ivegate, 1906.* An ancient Ivegate hostelry, the Old Crown was renowned for its tiny rooms, low ceilings and narrow corridors. In the early nineteenth century it provided rooms for those who were none too fussy about home comforts. Its reputation did not improve when it became a music hall. Here, mine host Bill Richardson stands at the door of the dram shop which he had converted from a window corner. Next door is Tommy Wardle's, retailer of pans, kettles, fenders, scuttles, tin baths and fire-irons.

53. *Bridge Street circa 1860.* Bradford's ancient horse-fair was traditionally held in Bridge Street on the day of St. Andrew the Apostle. When the Corporation purchased the manorial rights in 1866 they prohibited street fairs of this kind. At the far end of Bridge Street on the left is the home-trade warehouse of Milligan & Forbes close to the Exchange Railway Station.

54. *James Street vegetable market circa 1910.* A wholesale fruit and vegetable market opened in July 1874 for sale of vegetables, flowers as well as fish and poultry. Within the market site were two banks and the offices of two railway companies as well as a Post Office. In 1922 an extension was added at the rear of Diamond Street.

55. *Busby's original premises, Kirkgate.* A famous Bradford store whose recent passing saddened many local shoppers. The store was founded in these premises at the top of Albion Court in Kirkgate. Ernest William Busby opened the drapery store in 1908 and can be seen in frock coat in front of the shop. The firm vacated these premises in 1930 and moved to their more familiar Manningham Lane site in the same year.

56. *Interior Kirkgate Market.* Stalls of the 'Spice Market' should bring back fond memories for many Bradfordians. Here the flower stall of Messrs. Badlands (right) which confronted the market shopper once he had climbed the numerous steps at the Kirkgate entrance. In the corner, a favourite toy shop of the author's, where my grandma bought many a lead soldier and model car. Many will recall the second-hand book business of Mr. Fred Power, the sheet music stall not far away and the numerous pokey cafés, all selling pie and peas, tripe and onions, cornish pasty and chips, ideal fare on a cold Saturday shopping day.

57. *Swan Arcade, 1900.* Built on the site of the Old White Swan Inn, the arcade was designed by the architects Milnes & France and was completed in 1877. It fronted Market Street, Charles Street and Brook Street and its imposing archways and iron gates made many people think that it was private property in the early days. Its palatial accommodation included forty-four shops, a similar number of offices and numerous market rooms and warehouses.

58. *The corner shop.* An important social nexus for the mothers and housewives of the working-class street. But it wasn't all gossip and scandalmongering. Here, mines of information could be tapped on household economies, tasty recipes, tips on baby care and many other hints of domestic economy. The shop itself was a boon to the poorer housewife for here she could buy half a loaf, a pennorth of tea and the occasional luxury of a kipper or cow heel. In the last resort she was forced to take out a 'tick' book. Many a corner-shop owner decided which families should eat and which should not when times were hard.

59. *Sunbridge Road, circa 1920.* To the right of the picture are the Prudential Buildings which housed, amongst others, Edward Bush & Co., the optician and the London Tailoring Company. The corporation authorised the Duckworth Lane route as No. 8 (extreme left) in 1919. The double-decker trams with a seating capacity of 51 were built in 1903 and restructured in the years immediately following the First World War.

60. *Laisterdyke Toll Bar 1878.* An ancient and redundant bar house on the Dudley Hill - Killinghall - Harrogate Turnpike Trust which had been approved by parliament as early as 1736. Not all Bradfordians approved of this new system of road maintenance for in 1753 there were violent scenes at several local turnpike bars and gates where keepers were assaulted and gates burnt.

61. *Five Lane Ends.* The tram terminus at Five Lane Ends, Bank Top between Idle and Eccleshill.

62. *Bradford Canal.* The canal, leading off to the left of the photograph, was built in 1774 to connect the centre of Bradford to the main navigation of the Leeds-Liverpool Canal. This photograph shows the junction of the two canals at Dockfield, Shipley. The whitewashed building is that of Robinson's the boat builders.

63. *Exchange Railway Station, circa 1895.* The passenger terminal was completed in 1888 following the closure of Adolphus Street Station in 1867. An impressive building, but mostly hidden from view by stuff warehouses in Leeds Road. Its ten platforms were shared by the Great Northern Railway and the Lancashire & Yorkshire Railway companies. The station was spanned by two fine semi-circular roof arches (each 100 feet wide) and supported by ornamental wrought iron pillars. Its splendour failed to impress Bradford travellers whose main access was by the dark and dingy staircase entrance from Leeds Road.

64. *Midland Railway Station.* In contrast, this station (now Forster Square) has a much more prominent and central position. The station is lofty, light and airy as the roof is made entirely of glass and iron. The station replaced the buildings in the lower photograph when it was built in 1889/90.

65. *Midland Station and Hotel, 1906.* When opened in March 1890, the Midland Station and Hotel ranked as one of the leading railway centres in the country. The scheme had first been mooted in 1874 but railway revenues would not permit the immediate construction of such an ambitious project. It took five years to build and cost over a million pounds. The station had six platforms, well equipped rooms and was lit by electricity throughout. It was directly linked to the hotel whose main entrance was in Kirkgate. The five storey hotel had initially sixty bedrooms, all impressively furnished.

66. *Manchester Road* and its junction with Mayo Avenue in 1900.

67. *Old Clayton.* These are the premises of Sam Riley, the Royal Hotel in Clayton Lane.

68. *Scott's school, Low Moor.* Built by the owners of the Low Moor Ironworks close to Wibsey Chapel in 1814, it takes its name from the schoolmaster, John Scott, who taught here between 1832 and 1876. He was succeeded by his son of the same name, both taught the 3 R's to the children of foundrymen and colliers.

69. *Eastbrook Hall.* The new hall was opened in March 1904 by Mr. & Mrs. W. Oddy (centre) of Birkenshaw. Some thought the building too big but in February of 1905, 6,500 people attended for worship on a single Sunday. Next to Mr. Oddy (top hat) is Herbert Neild, who was Superintendent of Bradford Wesleyan Mission between 1903 and 1911.

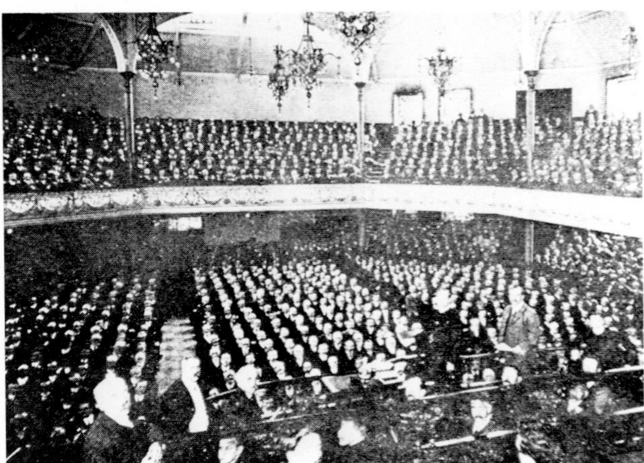

70. *Eastbrook Brotherhood.* The Eastbrook Brotherhood became the model for Men's Meetings everywhere after its foundation by Reverend H.M. Nield in September 1904. Nield's successor in 1911 was Reverend G.G. Muir and in spite of the war, the Brotherhood continued to thrive. Muir attracted to the Brotherhood many celebrated speakers including A. Conan Doyle, Lord Bishop of Bradford, Gypsy Smith and here in the second photograph, Rt. Hon. Arthur Henderson prepares to address the Brotherhood in 1920.

71. *Wilson's Restaurant, Kirkgate. 1920.* Wilson's were originally corn dealers in the town but became noted for their confectionery and restaurant in the late nineteenth century. Their ancient bow-fronted premises were demolished in 1920 to make way for the Anglo-South American Bank which was a British institution founded in 1889 to encourage the nitrate trade with Chile. Bradford spinners requiring raw wool were increasingly turning to the Argentine Republic, Uruguay and South Brazil for their supplies and to Peru and Bolivia for alpaca wool.

72. *Newlands Mill Chimney Fall, 1882.* This was the scene of Bradford's worst disaster on a site between Ripley Street and Upper Castle Street, off Manchester Road. For some days before the fall there had been fears that it was in danger of collapsing. It fell at nine o'clock on the morning of 28th December 1882. Most of the mill occupants had just settled down to their breakfasts. In addition to the seventy injured, fifty-three bodies were taken from the devastated area over the six days following the disaster. Many of them were teenage mill girls whose parents had great difficulty in identifying them.

73. *Theatre Royal, 1905.* The theatre opened Boxing Day 1864 as the Royal Alexandra, as there was already a Theatre Royal in Duke Street. It finally took that name in 1868 when its reputation soared under the management of Charles Rice. Although more famous for its pantomimes, many of the prominent Victorian stage names walked the theatre's boards. Lily Langtry appeared for a week in 1882, the fact that the Prince of Wales was opening the Bradford Technical College that very week was perhaps coincidental. The theatre is well known for its link with the death of Henry Irving (below), who fell ill in the theatre whilst playing 'Becket' and died shortly afterwards at the Midland Hotel. (Interior of the Midland Hotel.)

74. *Rydall Street, Bowling.* A street now demolished, but this scene is dominated by the West Bowling Wesleyan Chapel and Sunday Schools which had been built in 1888.

75. *Work people's housing.* Even when the town was municipalised in 1847, the abuses perpetrated in the name of housebuilding continued for three decades more. Hasty improvisation, in the form of back to back cottages, discounted any possibility of controlled planning. As late as 1921, the city had almost 41,000 back to back houses (54.4 per cent of total dwellings) and 3,700 of them were unfit for human habitation. The post-war demand for accommodation ensured that most of them were lived in. Only after the war was a programme of standardised municipal housing commenced.

76. *Chimney Sweep, 1890.* An all too frequent sight in Bradford in the late Victorian period when all houses were insulated by the coal fire.

77. *Laikin' Aht.* Many Edwardian working-class parents continued to regard it as a natural right that children should go out to work as soon as possible to compensate them for the 'kept' years of childhood. But it was good while it lasted and some Bradfordians look back with fondness upon the street games and songs they enjoyed as children. With their domestic chores done, the kids gathered together at some accepted place in the street, a lamp-post, covered alley or even a manhole cover. Here the towering backcloth of the mill and its chimney flanked by the proximity of the houses provides an unusually safe playground for these children.

78. *'Taws'.* A break for two Bradfordian errand boys at the turn of this century. They are playing taws, marbles or glass alleys. Most boys of the lower classes held part time jobs long before they left school. As unofficial errand boys they gathered round railway and omnibus stations, telegraph offices and large hotels. They fetched and carried for building labourers, mill workers and foundrymen. They were abused and exploited by a few employers but the majority of these lads earned important shillings for the family income, sometimes treating themselves to a copy of 'Magnet', 'Gem' or 'Union Jack'.

79. *Bradford school children 1908.* It was children like these, who were rescued by the progressive social work of Margaret Macmillan. In Bradford Board Schools she found children in every stage of neglect and suffering. The situation in the city's voluntary schools, like the Church School featured here, was no better. Bradford's first school medical inspection was held at Usher Street School in 1899 and by 1908 three and a half thousand Bradford school children were being inspected annually by the city's medical staff.

80. *School kitchen, Green Lane, 1908.* Since the Education Act of 1906 which Bradfordians had done much to prompt, the Bradford Education Authority provided free dinners and breakfasts for many of its children. A Central Kitchen was fitted up at Green Lane School and before the First World War was catering for 3,000 meals a day. Here, some tasty meat and potato pies are being prepared by kitchen staff at the municipal centre.

81. *Cleanliness is next to godliness, 1904.* Once you have cut through the happy gloss of community spirit, life in working-class Victorian Bradford was essentially dirty. Rubbish piles festered for months in back alleys where underfed cats and dogs roamed in search of the next meal only to find death, and then lie unmoved for weeks on end. Bradford's street urchins were thankful for the introduction of municipal baths where children in need of a bath could obtain one free of charge when taken by their teacher.

82. By 1922 the Bradford Corporation Health Department maintained a staff of fourteen Health Visitors who covered all twenty-one wards of the city. Each was a trained nurse and certificated midwife. They became well known in the local communities and visited children in the early years of their lives. They helped working-class mothers with information and advice, occasionally referring children to the Infant Clinic (opened 1912) for medical treatment.

83. *School P.E.* The end of the School Board era paved the way for an opening up of the elementary school curriculum. In 1909 the Central Board of Education issued a new P.E. syllabus of free-standing exercises which Bradford elementary schools took up immediately. Secondary schools were allowed to employ apparatus and here boys at Lilycroft School (built 1874) are training with dumb bells.

84. *The daily drop.* The Beerhouses Act of 1830 allowed any householder to sell beer on his premises on payment of a small fee. As a result the number of retail outlets for drink increased many times in Victorian cities like Bradford. Drink was an integral part of working-class culture and the corner public house became a common feature of working-class community life. Here, the working man found more than his daily intake of alcohol. The pub offered warmth, music, bright-lights, companionship, debate and a hint of sexuality if the landlady was bosomey enough. Draymen here deliver beer barrels to the premises of a back street pub (not known) in the Leeds Road area of Bradford in 1902.

85. *The New Inn.* Situated at the end of Tyrrel Street since the 1750's. This pub was the venue of Bradford's first flower show in August, 1827. In the early nineteenth century the pub was noted for its own pig market in the spacious stable yard at the rear. This modernised building may be remembered as it was only demolished in the clearance of Manchester Road in the 1960's. At the rear to the right is the familiar tower of the New Victoria Cinema (now Odeon One and Two).

86. *St. George's Hall circa 1880.* This was one of the solutions to Bradford's declining moral condition in the 1840's, according to the highly principled city fathers of the time (many of them Nonconformists) who viewed, with distaste, the working-class preference for brothels and singing rooms attached to public houses. The building was opened in September 1853 after a design by Lockwood & Mawnson. This magnificent concert hall has continued to be the city's main cultural forum. Here, curious passers-by stop to pose for the photographer.

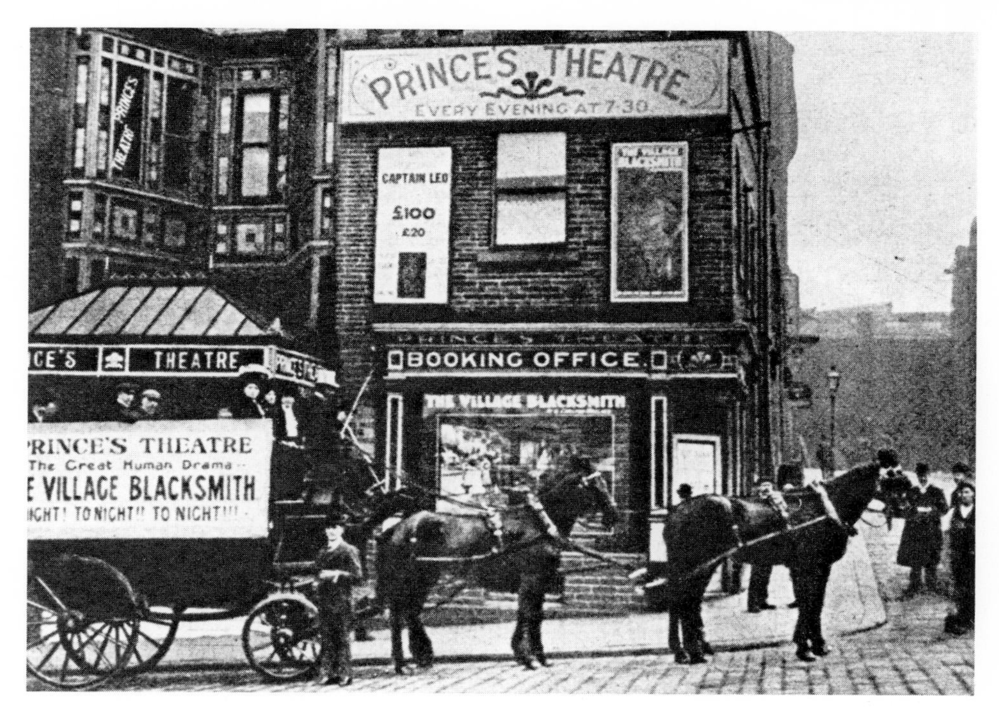

87. *The Princes Theatre, Manchester Road.* This well remembered place of entertainment was launched in 1875 by William Morgan, an early Bradford impresario of the late Victorian era. Two years later it was devastated by fire and had a precarious existence until 1886 when it was taken over by Henry Pullan and later by Francis Laidler, the King of Pantomime. It continued to provide live theatre until 1964 when it was demolished for the urban redevelopment programme. Bradfordians of today will recall the Princes as a fine repertory theatre which premiered several of Priestley's early plays. Underneath the Princes were the premises of the People's Palace, formerly the Star Music Hall. The Palace provided traditional music hall acts, comedians, illusionists etc. until its closure in May, 1938.

88. *The Alhambra.* This photograph was taken shortly before the outbreak of the First World War in 1914 when the Alhambra was opened by Francis Laidler on this site, as a variety theatre in direct competition with the Empire Theatre (opened 1899) which was built to the rear of the Alexandra Hotel (right of picture).

89. *Aladdin at the Alhambra.* A unique photograph from a performance of the pantomime 'Aladdin' in 1938. Here, that celebrated inter-war Northern comedian, Frank Randall, goes through his 'old Hiker' routine proclaiming that he 'wouldn't like to go up there on a bike' referring to the backcloth of the stage.

90. *Leeds Road circa 1910.* The electric tram is about to pass the Junction Hotel on the left of the picture and is approaching the recently built Eastbrook Hall (centre right). The photograph is interesting because of the lamp-post advertising Hibbert's Picture House in Chapel Street. Henry Hibbert was one of the pioneers of 'moving pictures'. He was, by trade, a dealer in game and fish with a keen interest in photography. His hobby took him all over the world and he was eventually made a Fellow of the Royal Geographical Society. The premises referred to in this photograph were Hibbert's 'picture' house at the Bradford Temperance Hall (opened 1903), where he showed his own films (Captain Kettle Film Co.) and those of other local pioneers in the business. The photographer was another local pioneer, Christopher Pratt, of Bradford's famed home-furnishing business.

91. *Dick Hudson's.* By name the Fleece Inn, High Eldwick, but better known to Bradfordians as Dick Hudson's as they poured out of their working city in their thousands on Good Friday or Whit Monday in Victorian times to find a brief sanctuary from the noise and smell of the weaving shed, or the heat and clamour of the iron furnace. A Bank Holiday trip to the watering-spa of Ilkley via Rombalds Moor, was the vacational treat for many Bradford workpeople. Their journey was enriched by the gourmet delights of dinner and tea at Dick Hudson's, a half-way house in each direction; best English beef and Yorkshire puddings at lunchtime and an enormous helping of ''am 'n' eggs' on the return journey.

92. *Bradford Super-Mare.* This is the promenade at Morecambe before 1914. Known as Bradford by the Sea for the number of Bradford people who holidayed there. The town's working-class families queued in their thousands at the Midland Station for excursion trains to Morecambe particularly on the Bowling Tide Saturday in August.

93. *Bradford city cup-winners 1911.* This success came only in the eighth season of the club's existence, having been promoted from Division Two in 1908. Almost 40,000 spectators paid their sixpences to watch City beat Burnley in the quarter-final at Valley Parade. A surprise 3-0 victory over Blackburn Rovers gave them a place in the final against cup favourites Newcastle United. Supporters from eleven excursion trains were disappointed by a goalless draw at Crystal Palace. The replay at Old Trafford the following Wednesday enabled ten thousand Bradfordians to see their team (including eight Scots) beat Newcastle by a Jimmy Spiers header. Spiers is seated immediately left of the F.A.-Cup with Secretary Peter O'Roarke standing far left.

94. *The Court House, Hall Ings, 1946.* The demolition of this building in 1958 caused a conservation controversy. It was an elegant three-storeyed structure erected in 1834 in the Grecian style. From beneath its striking portico Bradford's parliamentary candidates would address the town's voting population. The Exchange Station is in the background.

95. *The Packing department of a Bradford mill, circa 1910.* In 1901 over 57,000 Bradfordians were employed in textile manufacture. The majority of women worked in the spinning and weaving departments of the city's mills. Sorting, combing and dyeing chiefly employed men. Before 1914, Bradford is thought to have handled, in some way or other, five sixths of the wool in this country. Every wool transaction, from exporting the raw material to retailing the finished piece, was dealt with in Bradford. In 1910, the City's annual turnover in textiles was estimated at ninety million pounds.

96. *Well Street.* This busy and commercial thoroughfare has recently been transformed into a quiet inner-city backwater by the Petergate development. The street was first constructed in 1824 as part of the original Eastbrook House estate and the hillslope behind it developed after 1855 into the warren of narrow streets and shipping warehouses known as 'Little Germany'.

Well Street. This is one of the most imposing buildings in the warehouse precinct of 'Little Germany'. This magnificent façade along Well Street was built in 1867 and was designed by Eli Milnes. This post-war photograph, criss-crossed by the many overhead trolleybus wires of this busy junction, shows the headquarters of the Bradford Dyers' Association, a combination of Bradford master dyers founded in 1898.

97. *'Little Germany'.* This roof-top view overlooks the distinct and unique warehousing area of Bradford's Victorian worsted textile industry. From these buildings the city's merchant princes controlled an important export industry. Bottom left can be seen the east end of the old Parish Church (Cathedral) before the extensions of the 1960's. In the foreground is the junction of Peckover Street and Barkerend Road. Most of the warehouses in the picture were built in the early 1860's when business boomed. Through the smog, in the distance, you can just pick out the heavy arched roof of the Exchange railway station.

98. *Canal Road, 1890.* At the junction of North Brook Street with the vitriol works (founded 1750) in the background. The horses are just leaving the smithy premises of Billy Warhurst. In the distance can be seen the warehouse premises of the Leeds-Liverpool Canal Company. Only recently had the Bradford canal terminus been resited there.

Canal Road Warehouses. The Bradford Canal terminus was relocated on this site in 1867 as a result of the health hazard caused by the condition of the original canal basin below the Parish Church. These warehouses were jointly owned by the Leeds-Liverpool Company and the Aire-Calder Navigation Company. The last boat to deliver wool here was the steamer 'Beta' in 1921 when the canal was closed.

99. *Kirkgate circa 1900.* A late Victorian view up Kirkgate with the premises of the Bradford Banking Company (now the Midland Bank) to the right. The original premises were opened in 1828. The quality architecture of the bank is continued in the Kirkgate Market building (centre) opened in 1871. Across the road is the entrance to the narrow thoroughfare of Queensgate.

100. *Works outing.* Titus Salt was one of the first Bradford employers to get workmen and their employers pulling in the same direction after the industrial upheavals of the 1840's. In 1849 he took his millworkers to Skipton on the new railway. Here, Christopher Pratt, furniture manufacturers and retailers, treat their joinery staff to a day-out at Bolton Abbey in 1876.

A PICNIC GROUP AFTER BEN TILLETT'S CANDIDATURE FOR BRADFORD W. 1892
Extreme right—Ben Turner (delegate at 1893 Conference) and Mrs. Turner.
Centre—Mrs. Jowett, F. W. Jowett, Mrs. Til'ett (with child), Ben Tillett.
On ground at left—W. H. Drew.

101. *Ben Tillett's picnic group.* The Manningham Mills strike of 1891 precipitated the working men of Bradford into creating a political organisation of their own, the Bradford Labour Union. Unlike the Labour Electoral Association this new body refused to work within the Liberal party and put forward their own candidate, Ben Tillett for Bradford West in the general election of 1892. Tillett ran a creditable third but the Labour Union (renamed Bradford Independent Labour Party) had been established as a positive political force. Here, Tillett, his family and supporters relax during the election campaign.

THE FIRST NATIONAL COUNCIL OF THE I.L.P.
Back Row (left to right)—A. Field, J. Kennedy, J. Lister (Treasurer).
Centre Row (left to right)—G. S. Christie, J. W. Buttery, Joseph Burgess, W. H. Drew, E. Aveling, Alf Settle
W. Johnson, W. Small, Chisholm Roberton, George Carson.
Seated (left to right)—Pete Curran, Shaw Maxwell (Secretary), K. St. John Conway.

102. *Formation of I.L.P. in Bradford 1893.* The success of the Bradford Labour Union in 1892 confirmed its leadership of the labour movement and Bradford was consequently the venue of an inaugural conference of the national party in January 1893. In the photograph the newly elected national council of the Independent Labour Party stands before the Labour Institute in Peckover Street. Shaw Maxwell, former chairman of the Scottish Labour Party, was elected secretary and John Lister of Shibden Hall, Halifax, became treasurer.

103. *Cartwright Hall.* Situated in the city's most popular park, Lister Park. The hall was built on the site of Lord Masham's first family home. He gave £47,000 for its erection as a permanent monument to Dr. Edmund Cartwright, a pioneering inventor of the power-loom and wool combing machine. Until recent years it served as the city's central museum as well as a botanical garden.

104. *Somali Village, Bradford Exhibition, 1904.* The aged Lord Masham had officially opened the Cartwright Memorial Hall in April 1904. The Inaugural Exhibition commenced 4th May of that year and was opened by the Prince and Princess of Wales (afterwards King George V and Queen Mary). One of the many highlights of the exhibition was a real Somali village inhabited by natives of that country. For months they were continuously a public spectacle, several of their huts burnt down and a number of them died in this strange land.

105. *The Victoria Statue.* Later in 1904 the Prince and Princess of Wales returned to Bradford for the unveiling of Queen Victoria's statue. A gallery had been specially erected for the occasion and three thousand Bradford school children sang for the royal guests. Brilliant sunshine, the colour and noise of military bands, brought 50,000 Bradfordians into the city centre that day. Backcloth to the photograph is the Horton Lane Congregational Chapel.

106. *Bradford and The Declaration of War 1914.* The Sixth Battalion West Yorkshire Regiment was mobilised on August 4th, 1914. Four days later a thousand local men had responded to fight for 'king and country'. As E635 they were assembled at Belle Vue Barracks. Here, outside the barracks and adjoining the pub, the news first breaks of the declaration of war.

Mobilisation. A week later the batallion left the barracks at the crack of dawn. Their early morning march to the Midland Railway Station was viewed by solitary passers-by and a handful of workers on the early shift. There was no cheering, no acclaim, none of the razzamatazz which had accompanied the lads departing for the Boer War.

107. *Reading room, Bradford Library 1922.* For the ranks of the unemployed in the inter-war years Bradford Library's reading room in Darley Street was a favourite haunt. The city's first public library had opened in Tyrrel Street in 1872. Six years later it transferred to new premises in the Kirkgate Market precinct. Within a decade this accommodation was inadequate but there was no further move until 1966.

108. *Town Hall Square 1926.* At the junction of Thornton Road (centre) and Tyrrell Street (right).

109. *Market Street circa 1935.* A view of the junction of Market Street with Town Hall Square. On the left are the former premises of the Bradford Third Equitable Benefit Building Society and the hosiery shop of Miss Skelton which the Queensbury tram is about to pass.

110. *Midland Hotel and Forster Square 1935.* This is Forster Square leading to Kirkgate in the distance. Beyond the Midland Hotel (1885) with its octagonal dome-topped tower are the premises of the Bank built in 1885 and designed by Milnes & France in a classical style.

Forster Square 1933. A similar view looking from the junction of Cheapside and Kirkgate. Tram lines and overhead cables indicate the 'dual' public transport system of tram and trolleybus. Bradford was the first authority in the country to introduce the trackless trolleybus in 1911, but it was not until 1923 that the system was popularised with the use of balloon tyres and electrically powered buses.

111. *John Street Market 1950.* An open market built in 1931. In all there were 175 stalls and shops, a good proportion of them covered. To the right of the picture were several herbalists' stores which gave the market its nickname of 'Quack Market'.

112. *Rawson Place Market circa 1920.* The butchers' portion was opened on 13th November 1875 and the extension to John Street completed thirty years later. The total cost was over £98,000 and provided 74 stalls and shops.

113. *Unitarian Chapel, Chapel Lane, circa 1900.* Two views looking towards the Unitarian Chapel across Town Hall Square. The chapel was resited here in 1869 and provided sitting for five hundred people. Next door to the chapel are the premises of S. Dalby, fine art dealer, and H.J. Knutton, sports outfitters.

114. *Darley Street, 1935.* This district was originally part of the manorial estate, that is the gardens, orchards, and rockery. It had a reputation in 1900 for being the city's fashionable thoroughfare. Below the Kino's sign was the bookshop of Mr. Wilson and on the right of Darley Street can be discerned the Savoy Cinema where the first 'talkie', Al Jolson's 'Singin' Fool', was shown in 1929.

115. *North Parade, 1930.*

116. *Yorkshire Penny Bank, 1935.* This inter-war photograph shows Manningham Lane at the junction with North Parade and Manor Row. In the centre of the photograph are the premises of the Yorkshire Penny Bank dominated by the strikingly oriental clock tower.

117. *The New Victoria Cinema.* As mentioned elsewhere Bradford men had done much to pioneer the creation of moving films in the last decade of the nineteenth century, but the real cinema boom occurred in the 1920's. This splendid new cinema was built in 1930 on the site of an old brewery. It housed an enormous organ, the Mighty Wurlitzer, and the cinema could seat over three thousand people.

118. *Bradford Whit. Walk, 1954.* This occasion has provided Bradfordians with a cultural and sporting event for their traditional Whit Monday holiday since 1903 when Len Atkinson of Baildon was the first to complete the route to York (39½ miles) in just over seven hours. Here we see the start of the race in 1954 with the prominent backcloth of the Ritz cinema in Broadway. The Yorkshire Walking Club was formed in Bradford in June 1912 under the presidency of Mr. J. Russell Rose.

119. The final photographs in this book depict a Bradford that has now gone, lost in the rush of urban redevelopment in the years after the Second World War. And yet it is a Bradford strong in the minds of many of its citizens today. The blackened buildings and depressing streets which prevail in these photographs still smacked of the 'dark satanic mill' environment of the Victorian age and were not conducive to a new and better Bradford after 1945. They had to go. For us they survive in this brief pictorial record.

Here is *Broadway* in 1947. For many years this area was cleared for redevelopment (front left) but inter-war city councils dragged their feet. The one new building, a striking architectural innovation for the city, was the Ritz cinema. To the left can be seen the Swan Arcade, a favourite haunt of the young J.B. Priestley.

120. *Darley Street, 1947.* Few changes have taken place to the foreground of this picture apart from the car designs of course but in the distance is the Institute for the Blind. The building furthest from the camera is that of the furnishers, Christopher Pratt & Sons in North Parade.

121. *Forster Square, 1947.* Rush-hour queues for the trolleybus service to Nab Wood and Saltaire. In the background a 'mixed' architectural scene with the Victorian mills and warehouses of North Wing, the General Post Office and the intruding tower of the Cathedral.

122. *Britannia House, Bridge Street.* A popular 'rendezvous' point and well known even today's generation of Bradfordians. This building was constructed on the site of the old Cuckoo Bridge and was opened in 1927. Its tidy style and sophisticated stonework are perhaps impaired by the rather pathetic attempt at a dome.

123. *Ivegate, 1947.* A Bradford highway which has experienced few changes in the years since the Second World War, Ivegate's narrowness and steepness made it an obvious early choice as a one way street. To the far right are the premises of the Prudential Assurance Company and the District Bank while on the opposite side of the road is Thorpe Building, the home of Barclay's Bank. The Unicorn Hotel and the Old Crown Hotel face each other in lower Ivegate.

124. *Manningham Lane.* The motor car became the symbol of the consumer society in the years after the Second World War. By 1947, when this photograph was taken, there were over two million cars in use in Great Britain. The car transformed this ancient Bradford highway as it led westwards to the growing dormer towns of Baildon, Shipley and Bingley. The leisure boom of the late nineteenth century located several of its important venues in this direction. Bradford City played at Valley Parade and close by was the Belle Vue Skating Rink as well as the Valley Parade Rink. Several of these rinks were later converted into cinemas as was the Theatre Royal which is featured here. The building on the right housed the Independent Order of Rechabites and top left can be seen the Connaught Rooms.